The INSIDE GUIDE

STEM IN SPORTS

STEM in Gymnastics

By Beatrice Harris

Cavendish Square

Published in 2025 by Cavendish Square Publishing, LLC
2544 Clinton Street Buffalo, NY 14224

Website: cavendishsq.com

Library of Congress Cataloging-in-Publication Data

Names: Harris, Beatrice, author.
Title: STEM in gymnastics / Beatrice Harris.
Description: Buffalo, New York : Cavendish Square Publishing, [2025] | Series: The inside guide: STEM in sports | Includes index.
Identifiers: LCCN 2023050941 (print) | LCCN 2023050942 (ebook) | ISBN 9781502671349 (library binding) | ISBN 9781502671332 (paperback) | ISBN 9781502671356 (ebook)
Subjects: LCSH: Gymnastics–Juvenile literature. | Science–Study and teaching–Juvenile literature. | Sports sciences–Juvenile literature.
Classification: LCC GV461.3 .H37 2025 (print) | LCC GV461.3 (ebook) | DDC 796.44–dc23/eng/20231101
LC record available at https://lccn.loc.gov/2023050941
LC ebook record available at https://lccn.loc.gov/2023050942

Editor: Therese Shea
Copyeditor: Danielle Haynes
Designer: Deanna Lepovich

The photographs in this book are used by permission and through the courtesy of: Cover, pp. 18, 21 Real Sports Photos/Shutterstock.com; p. 4 Anders Riishede/Shutterstock.com; p. 6 Artur Didyk/Shutterstock.com; p. 7 (icons) ID-EasyDoor/Shutterstock.com; pp. 9, 28 (bottom) PeopleImages.com - Yuri A/Shutterstock.com; p. 10 Air Images/Shutterstock.com; pp. 12, 20 Salty View/Shutterstock.com; p. 13 (top) Luigi Fardella/Shutterstock.com; p. 13 (bottom) Rawpixel.com/Shutterstock.com; p. 15 Jiang Dao Hua/Shutterstock.com; pp. 16, 22, 24, 25 Alex Bogatyrev/Shutterstock.com; p. 19 roibu/Shutterstock.com; p. 26 Laoongjune/Shutterstock.com; p. 27 I T A L O/Shutterstock.com; p. 28 (top) Victor Velter/Shutterstock.com; p. 29 (top) Leonard Zhukovsky/Shutterstock.com; p. 29 (bottom) Juice Dash/Shutterstock.com.

CPSIA compliance information: Batch #CSCSQ25: For further information contact Cavendish Square Publishing LLC at 1-877-980-4450.

Printed in the United States of America

CONTENTS

Many consider Simone Biles to be the best gymnast of all time. To reach the top of her sport, she had to be dedicated and smart.

Chapter One

A STEM SPORT

Gymnastics is one of the most popular sports in the world and the athletes who compete at the highest level are some of the most admired. Gymnastics requires strength, **flexibility**, balance, and endurance—and let's not forget STEM (science, **technology**, engineering, and math)! That might sound funny, but it's true. Gymnasts need to understand the STEM ideas behind the sport to perform their best in every event.

Artists at Work

There are three main kinds of gymnastics. Rhythmic gymnastics combines exercises with the use of ropes, hoops, clubs, balls, and ribbons. Trampolining or trampoline gymnastics is a kind of gymnastics that uses the bouncy mat as a springboard for various exercises. Artistic gymnastics, though, is perhaps the most famous.

> **Fast Fact**
>
> In all-around events, the scores of all the competition exercises are added together.

In artistic gymnastics, women usually take part in four events: floor exercise, uneven bars, vault, and balance beam. Men in artistic gymnastics often compete in six events: floor exercise, pommel horse, rings, vault, parallel bars, and

GOING FOR THE GOLD

Gymnastics is one of the most-watched sports at the Summer Olympics. It has been a part of the Olympics since the modern games began in 1896, although only men could participate in gymnastics until 1928. Now, every four years, people watch the best gymnasts in the world jump, flip, and twist their way through challenging events to win a medal. Gymnasts train for years to be good enough to secure a spot on their country's Olympic team. Famous gymnasts such as Nadia Comăneci, Gabby Douglas, and Simone Biles became familiar names partly because of their medal-winning Olympic routines.

Rhythmic gymnastics has elements of dance in it. It's beautiful to watch.

ARTISTIC GYMNASTICS EVENTS

Women's Events

uneven bars

balance beam

floor exercise

vault

Men's Events

pommel horse

rings

parallel bars

horizontal bar

floor exercise

vault

Both men and women compete in the floor exercise and vault, though they do not compete against each other in these events.

horizontal bar. Men and women each also compete in all-around exercises. In this book, we'll focus on STEM ideas in artistic gymnastics.

Scoring with Math

It might not be clear where gymnastics and math meet. Math comes into play in competition. After a gymnast completes an event, judges give them two sets of scores. The first is the difficulty score. Judges give every skill a certain point value. The judges add up the points for the gymnast's hardest skills in an event. The second score is the **execution** score. Judges start at 10 and then deduct points—ranging from 0.1 to 1.0—for mistakes. The highest and lowest judges' scores are thrown out, and the average score is the gymnast's execution score. Judges determine a gymnast's total score for an event by adding the difficulty score and execution score together.

Fast Fact

Judges include connection points in their difficulty scores. These are points awarded to gymnasts for putting hard skills together.

More Than One Science

Every gymnastics event is an example of science at work. Physics is a branch of science that deals with the interaction between matter and energy, including how objects move and the forces that act upon them. Physics can explain gymnasts' every motion—no matter how incredible.

Gymnasts also need a good understanding of anatomy and physiology. Both are branches of biology, the science of living things. Anatomy focuses on body structures, such as skin, muscles,

Fast Fact

Athletes need to know about nutrition, which is the study of food and how the body uses it. The body needs nutritious food for energy, muscle growth, bone health, and more.

Gymnasts need to care for their body to perform their best. That means understanding how it works, which can help prevent injuries.

bones, lungs, and the heart. Physiology is the study of how these body parts work. Knowing about these can help gymnasts not only train but also avoid injuries.

You can see a gymnast's muscles at work as they compete.

Chapter Two

BODY SCIENCE

Gymnasts aren't born skilled. They train hard to be the best in their sport. They use their knowledge of anatomy and physiology to increase their strength and flexibility.

Gymnasts stretch, or lengthen their muscles, to increase their flexibility. To get stronger muscles, they do exercises that increase their muscle mass. This is called muscular hypertrophy. Gymnasts especially want to build strong muscles in their legs and shoulders. They must be careful, however, not to increase the size of their muscles too much. That would increase their overall body mass, which would make it harder to compete in certain events.

Fast Fact

On Earth, mass and weight are used to mean the same thing. However, a person's weight has to do with the force of gravity on Earth and their mass has to do with the amount of matter that makes up their body. So, mass remains the same on any planet, but weight differs with gravity.

Around the Axis

Gymnastics and kinesiology are a good match. This branch of science studies body movements. People with a background in

A gymnast's body creates the forces necessary to execute routines. Muscles, tendons, and joints work with bones to generate force in the form of movement.

kinesiology might specialize in a sport such as gymnastics, training gymnasts and helping them understand the best way to perform a challenging routine.

One area of kinesiology involves the way a person's body rotates, or spins, around an axis. An axis is an imaginary line through the middle of an object. One of the axes in the human body is the frontal axis. This axis runs horizontally, or from side to side, through the body. A gymnast rotates around this axis when they do a somersault, or forward roll.

The longitudinal, or vertical, axis runs from the top of the body to the bottom. A gymnast rotates around this axis when they do a spin.

Knowing where a certain axis is in their body can help a gymnast think about how to perform a skill.

The third axis, called the sagittal or anteroposterior axis, runs from front to back through the body's center. A cartwheel rotates around the sagittal axis.

Gymnasts wow crowds by executing multiple rotations around one of their body's

To execute multiple rotations perfectly, gymnasts bring their body parts as close to the axis of rotation as possible.

Fast Fact

Another way to divide the body is in planes, which are imaginary flat surfaces running through the body.

THE TERRIBLE TWISTIES

Simone Biles withdrew from some Olympic events in 2021 because of what many gymnasts call "the twisties." She said she couldn't tell where her body was in the air. This "air sense" has to do with proprioception, an awareness of the body's movements. Some gymnasts have to go back to the basics of their training to get over the twisties. Biles overcame hers by practicing on a trampoline until it was "second nature again," she said. Two years later, she won four gold medals and a silver medal at the 2023 Artistic World Championships, becoming the most decorated gymnast ever. As of 2023, Biles had won 34 medals in world championship and Olympic competitions.

axes—often in midair. These rotations are measured in degrees. One full rotation is 360 degrees, so two would be twice that, or 720, and so on.

Fast Fact

No one is sure yet how to prevent the twisties. Picturing the movement in one's brain may help, as could lowering stress through deep breathing and other relaxation methods.

Aware, Even in the Air!

As gymnasts are tumbling across the floor or executing a flip on a beam, they need to be aware of their body's movements and position in space. This awareness is known as kinesthetic awareness or proprioception. It's a kind of sixth sense.

Gymnasts need to always know their body's position and motion. This awareness keeps them from falling off the balance beam or hurting themselves by moving a body part incorrectly.

Sensors, called proprioceptors, in muscles, joints, tendons, and other body parts send messages to the brain about those body parts. For example, these sensors send messages to the brain about the angle of the body's limbs, so the brain is aware of the body's motion. When a gymnast is in the middle of a flip, these sensors help their brain to recognize the position of body parts, even when the gymnast can't see for themselves.

Tumbling passes begin with a gymnast running across the floor, starting from one of its corners.

Chapter Three

ON AND ABOVE THE FLOOR

The floor exercise is one of the events in which a gymnast's skills really shine as they perform a routine consisting of flips, twists, and other elements. Tumbling passes are flips done in a series. They make up a key part of the floor exercise and are a great way to learn about speed, **velocity**, and **acceleration**.

Quick Change

When gymnasts run, they quickly change their position on the floor. The rate at which an object's position changes is known as its velocity. A gymnast's velocity increases as they run across the floor. This change in velocity is known as acceleration. Gymnasts start their tumbling passes at one corner of the floor, so they have as much room as possible to accelerate.

Fast Fact

Gymnasts must stay within a square for the floor exercise. Each side of the square measures 39.37 feet (12 meters) long.

Sometimes we talk about acceleration, velocity, and speed as if they have the same meaning. They are different, though. Direction doesn't matter when measuring speed, just distance and time. However, direction is a necessary

Positive acceleration—or an increasing velocity over a certain time—is needed for a gymnast to execute certain moves.

part of velocity and acceleration, both of which are figured out in part by how far an object is from its original position, not the overall distance traveled. This is called displacement.

Forces at Work

Forces are at work in the floor exercise. A force is a push or pull on an object, and forces are what help gymnasts get the power they need to execute their flips. This kind of force is called applied force. An applied force is a force **exerted** on an object, such as a gymnast's hands pushing off the floor before a flip. The acceleration of the running gymnast helps create the amount of force needed to accomplish the flip.

While applied force helps gymnasts push themselves into the air, gravity pulls them back down. Gravity is a force that pulls objects (and people) toward the center of Earth. People often say gymnasts are working against gravity because they try to stay in the air as long as possible before this force brings them back down to the mat or another piece of equipment.

The floor is exerting a force on this gymnast. The upward force that a surface applies to objects upon them is called normal force.

Fast Fact

Gravity is also the force that keeps the moon orbiting Earth and Earth orbiting the sun.

VIDEO REVIEW

An important technology that gymnasts and their coaches use is video. Video can allow gymnasts to see their **routines** and what they may need to work on. All those extremely fast flips and twists can make it hard for the gymnast to tell where they might be going wrong, so video can help them spot errors that judges might find fault with at a competition. Video can also shine a light on a gymnast's strengths. Judges might use video replay to watch a routine again if a coach disagrees with their scoring.

A judge looks on as Olympic gymnast Diego Hypólito competes in the floor exercise.

Special Spring Floors

The special floor used in the floor exercise helps gymnasts jump higher than normal and helps prevent injuries to their legs and feet. Engineers—people who use math and science to make technology—put springs underneath the top layers of the floor. Spring floors exert a kind of force called spring force on a gymnast's body. When a gymnast jumps on a spring floor, they push springs down. The springs then push back on the gymnast's feet with an upward force.

Fast Fact

Spring floors absorb some of the downward force applied by a gymnast as they land, which helps prevent injuries.

Spring floors are an example of technology in gymnastics.

When a gymnast flips off an apparatus, it's important for them to stick their landing or judges may deduct points.

STICKING THE LANDING WITH NEWTON

Chapter Four

Sticking the landing in gymnastics means landing on the ground without moving. Sticking a landing isn't easy, and physics explains why. Isaac Newton, a scientist who lived from 1643 to 1727, can help us understand why gymnasts may keep moving after they hit the ground.

Newton's Laws

Newton developed three basic laws of motion that apply to all objects in nature. Newton's first law of motion states that an object at rest stays at rest and an object in motion stays in motion unless acted on by an outside force. So, applying this to a gymnastics routine, when a gymnast's body is in motion, it wants to stay in motion. Stopping quickly to stick a landing takes a lot of force.

> **Fast Fact**
>
> Ideally, much of the force of a landing is absorbed into the padded landing surface. Landing on harder surfaces means more force is absorbed by the body, which can lead to injury.

Newton's second law of motion tells us that force is equal to mass multiplied by acceleration. So,

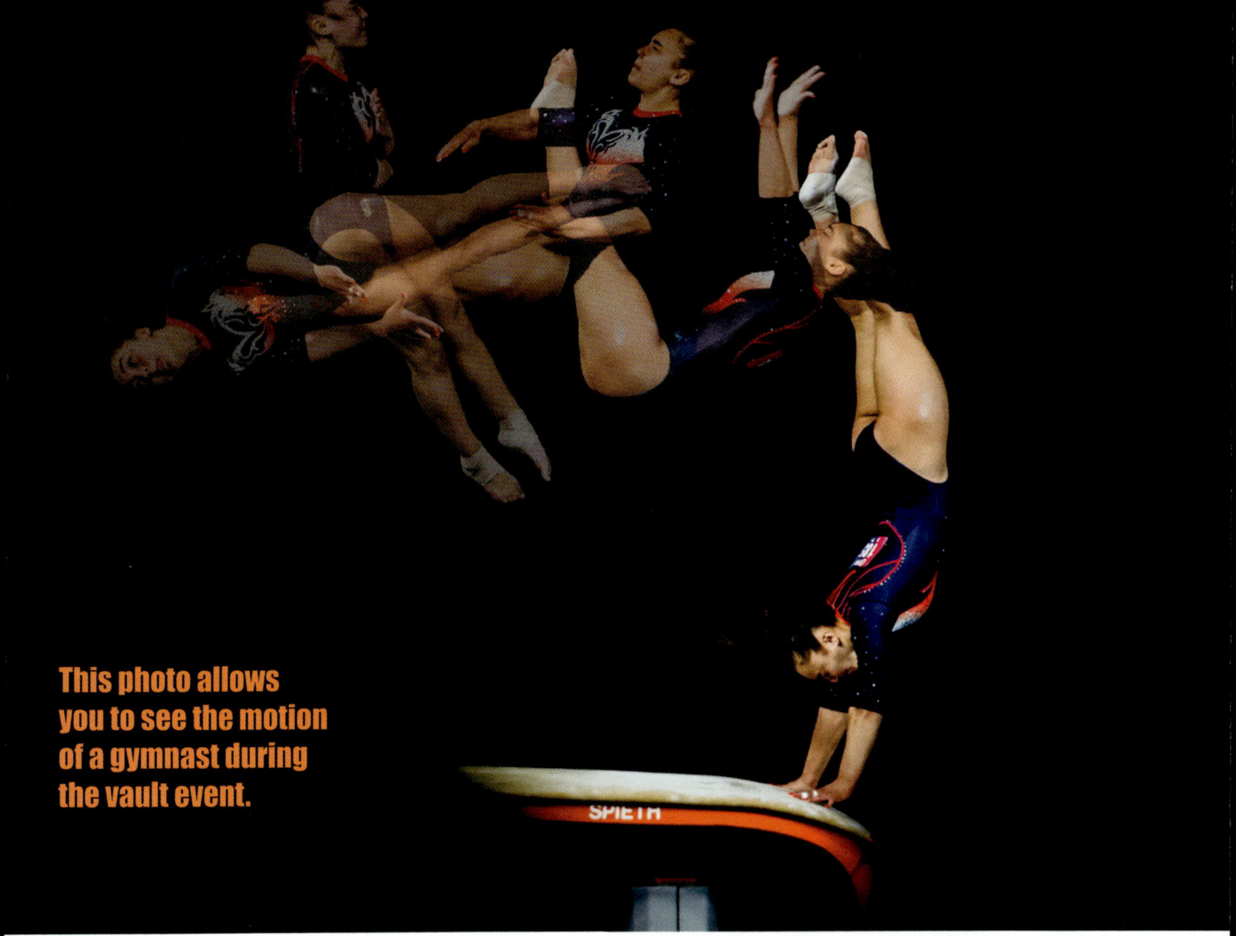

This photo allows you to see the motion of a gymnast during the vault event.

force increases when acceleration increases. However, acceleration decreases when the object's mass increases. Thus, a gymnast works to build muscle strength—but not body mass—to be able to create more force and acceleration.

Newton's third law of motion states that for every action, there's an equal and opposite **reaction**. This can be seen during the vault event. The gymnast runs toward a piece of equipment called a vaulting table. They jump onto a springboard, which allows them to push off

Fast Fact

In 2001, a vaulting table with a wider surface area was introduced to reduce injuries.

The front of the vaulting table is curved downward and covered with thick padding. It's nicknamed the tongue!

the table with their hands. Finally, they do a number of rotations in the air before landing.

When the gymnast jumps on the springboard, the springboard pushes them up toward the table with equal force. Then, when their hands push down on the table, the table pushes back on their hands with an equal, upward force.

The Force of Friction

Friction is one of the outside forces at work in Newton's first law. It acts on objects in motion. Friction provides resistance when an object moves

Gymnasts' hands can get sweaty. Sweat acts as a lubricant, which is a substance that reduces friction and makes things slippery. Some gymnasts use a mixture of chalk and water to prevent that slipperiness.

Fast Fact

Pancake syrup and melted gummy bears are sticky substances that gymnasts have used to help them get a better grip!

against another object, such as a gymnast running across a mat. Friction works to slow the object's motion, but it can be helpful too.

For instance, gymnasts don't want their hands to slip off the horizontal or uneven bars, so they use sticky substances to create more friction between their hands and the surface of the apparatus.

STEM for a Perfect 10!

Every gymnastics event is a STEM lesson. Science is behind forces and motion in all events. All apparatuses are examples of engineering and technology. Also, without math, the events couldn't be scored.

Next time you watch a gymnastics competition, watch for STEM ideas at work. You'll be even more amazed by the amount of skill and strength it takes for your favorite athlete to seem to **defy** gravity and stick the landing!

GRAVITY AND BALANCE

Gravity is always pulling down on gymnasts. A person's center of gravity is the imaginary point of their body where all their weight is in balance. A body with a lower center of gravity is easier to keep in balance than one with a higher center of gravity. This is why gymnasts bend their knees on the balance beam when they feel unsteady. That motion brings their center of gravity closer to the beam, making them more stable. A shorter person has a lower center of gravity, so shorter gymnasts often have an easier time keeping their balance than taller ones.

With every move, a person's center of gravity changes. Gymnasts learn to adjust their body so they don't lose their balance.

THINK ABOUT IT!

1. Choose one gymnastics event and explain how each part of STEM connects to it.

2. Explain how a knowledge of anatomy and physiology could help a gymnast prevent injury.

3. What challenges does a taller gymnast face in terms of physics?

4. Do you think gymnasts train differently than other athletes? How?

GLOSSARY

acceleration: The rate at which the velocity of an object in motion changes over time.

apparatus: A tool or object needed to perform in a gymnastic event.

dedicated: Giving time and attention to an activity.

defy: To resist or go against.

execution: The act of completing or performing.

exert: To put forth.

flexibility: The ability to bend easily.

reaction: The force that an object subjected to an outside force exerts in the opposite direction.

routine: A repeated series of activities or movements.

technology: Using science, engineering, and other industries to invent useful tools or to solve problems. Also, a machine, piece of equipment, or method created by technology.

tendon: A band of tough tissue that connects muscles and bones.

velocity: The speed and direction of a moving object.

FIND OUT MORE

Books

Havelka, Jacqueline. *STEM in Gymnastics*. Broomall, PA: Mason Crest, 2020.

Monnig, Alex. *Gymnastics*. Minneapolis, MN: A & D Xtreme, 2023.

Wood, Alix. *Gymnastics*. Buffalo, NY: Enslow Publishing, 2023.

Websites

Encyclopedia.com: Gymnastics Landing Forces
www.encyclopedia.com/sports/sports-fitness-recreation-and-leisure-magazines/gymnastics-landing-forces
Read more about sticking the landing in gymnastics.

Rookie Road: What Is Gymnastics?
www.rookieroad.com/gymnastics/what-is/
Rookie Road has tons of facts about this sport, its events, and rules.

***Smithsonian* Magazine: A History of Gymnastics**
www.smithsonianmag.com/history/history-gymnastics-ancient-greece-tokyo-2020-180978270/
Discover the long, interesting history of this beloved sport.

Publisher's note to educators and parents: Our editors have carefully reviewed these websites to ensure that they are suitable for students. Many websites change frequently, however, and we cannot guarantee that a site's future contents will continue to meet our high standards of quality and educational value. Be advised that students should be closely supervised whenever they access the internet.

INDEX